THE EMPEROR LAYS AN EGG

BRENDA Z. GUIBERSON
ILLUSTRATED BY JOAN PALEY

HENRY HOLT AND COMPANY · NEW YORK

In late May, as an icy winter wind blows across Antarctica, a mother emperor penguin lays an egg. *Plop!* To keep the egg from freezing, she catches it on her feet and covers it with a flap of skin.

Then *shuffle, shuffle, scoop*. The father uses his beak to quickly move the egg to his own feet. He cuddles it against the bare spot on his fat body. Tucked into his brood pouch, the egg is safe and warm.

The mother has not eaten for the six weeks since the penguins arrived at the breeding ground, or rookery. She is exhausted and hungry, but all around her the surface of the ocean has frozen into thick ice. To find something to eat, she must travel ninety miles to the open sea. With small, stiff wings, the emperor cannot fly, so she waddles in a line with other mothers at less than one mile an hour. *Waddle, waddle.* In the cold darkness she climbs up a bumpy slope and struggles around a long, jagged crack. Finally she sees a field of slick ice, and toboggans on her white belly to speed up the four-day trip. *Swoosh! Swoosh!*

All the other wild creatures have left the Antarctic. The wind is too cold and the sun does not shine during the long, dark months of winter. But the father emperor stays behind with thousands of other fathers. Each of them takes care of an egg, but none of them have a nest. Instead, they walk carefully, *shuffle, shuffle,* while they balance their eggs on their feet. It is such a strong instinct that one emperor who doesn't have an egg shuffles around with a chunk of ice about the size of a softball.

To save his energy during the first twenty days, the father stands as still as a fire hydrant on the very same spot of ice. His eighty-pound body is covered with curved feathers and a thick layer of blubber to keep him warm. There is nothing to eat, but he gets some energy as his body begins to use the blubber. *Howl . . . whoosh!* The cold wind blows snow against his tough feathers. As the snow swirls through the air, he drinks a mouthful.

Screech, whoooo! Now the wind blasts like a hurricane. It is cold enough to crack teeth and freeze water in the air. The emperor can no longer stay warm by himself. Thousands of penguins with eggs on their feet huddle together. The father is at the back of the group, where there is too much wind. *Shuffle, shuffle.* He moves slowly around to the front, for better shelter. Soon other birds move up to take his place. The temperature is minus 60 degrees Fahrenheit, but each emperor and his egg get a turn to warm up in the group. In spite of the careful shuffling, a few eggs break. But the father's egg stays safe and remarkably warm, at 98 degrees Fahrenheit.

In July, in the middle of the worst winter blizzard,
the emperor's egg is ready to hatch. *Chip, chip, crack!*
Out pops a bedraggled gray chick. The father lets the baby
peek out while he cleans up the shell, but then he tucks the
baby right back under. In the coldest, windiest, driest place on
Earth, the father has taken care of the egg for sixty-five days.
He is running out of energy. In his throat, he can make only
a small amount of the nutritious liquid called penguin's milk
to spit up for the baby. With the tiny emperor still on his feet,
the father waits and waits for the mother to return.

After another cold week, the father finally hears the trumpet song of his mate. *Toodoo, twoo!* In the frigid darkness, the mother waddles back from the sea with food for the baby. The father lets the tiny emperor out onto the ice. It is a dangerous moment. In just two minutes of exposure, the baby can freeze to death. *Whoosh . . . whish.* The chick shivers in the wind. But the mother scoops it up quickly and covers it with a warm flap of skin. The chick reaches into her throat to gobble the meal of fish and squid that she has spit up. She toodles to the baby and the baby whistles back as they learn each other's songs.

Now the father gets a vacation. He has not eaten for one hundred and fifteen days and has lost half his body weight. He is thin and dirty when he finally leaves the baby to walk across the ice. After the storm, so much of the sea is frozen that it takes him two weeks to find an opening. When he reaches the edge of the ice, he waits to dive in. *Gurgle, swish!* The water is churning. *Snap!* A leopard seal hunts for a meal of penguin.

When it is safe, the father leaps off the ice with the other hungry fathers. *Splish! Splash!* Now the emperor's wings work like powerful flippers and he swims like a torpedo. *Gulp, gulp, gulp!* He gobbles up fish and tiny shrimplike creatures called krill. Then he takes an incredible thousand-foot dive to find the squid that swim deep in the sea. After three weeks of eating, he has built up a new layer of blubber. *Splat!* He leaps out of the water and lands with a belly flop on the ice. He uses his beak to preen his feathers and then waddles toward the rookery with food for the baby.

Now the parents take turns caring for the chick. One parent keeps the baby warm, while the other travels to the sea. *Crack! Crack!* The ice in the rookery is stable, but all around it the frozen ocean shifts, splits, and refreezes. The emperors jump over crevices and climb slippery slopes to reach the water. As they travel back and forth, every meal they carry in their crops must be huge, as much as seven pounds of food. In five months of feeding the chick, they are able to return with only fourteen meals.

In August, the red sun returns to shimmer across the ice and warm the air. As the days lighten and the long winter comes to an end, the chick grows too large to sit on its parents' feet. It is time to leave the pouch, build up some muscles, and learn to waddle and toboggan. The chick stands close to a parent for warmth or huddles in a group with other chicks. All over the rookery, fluffy gray babies try out their sharp claws on the ice. A few of them wander off by themselves and are not able to survive a late-spring storm.

When the short summer begins, seals, sea birds, and whales return to raise their babies. There is plenty to eat, since the sun shining into the water starts a population explosion of algae, krill, and fish. The emperor parents spend more and more time in the water. By December, the three-foot-tall chick is on its own but is still unable to get food for itself. First the baby needs a new coat. Fluffy gray down falls out as black and white feathers grow in. With its waterproof feathers in place, the chick is ready for the ocean. The ice is breaking up and the young penguins find the open water all by themselves. *Splash, splash, splash.* One after another, they dive from a great icy cliff into the sea.

The mother and father fatten up again during the short summer, but their feathers have taken a beating. In February, as the emperors sit on a floating chunk of sea ice, they lose the old feathers and grow new ones. Packed tightly together like tiny roof tiles, there are eighty waterproof feathers in one square inch. During this molt, the penguins cannot survive in the water, so they spend several more weeks without a bite to eat. Patiently they wait for the shiny, oily new feathers that will protect them from the bitter cold.

By early April, the temperature of the autumn air is already down to minus 20 degrees Fahrenheit and the ocean begins to freeze quickly. As other creatures head north, the mother and father emperors waddle south. *Toodoo, twoo!* In the rookery, they trumpet and bow their heads along with thousands of other chattering penguins. The young chicks need six years to grow up, but the older birds are ready to mate. They are fat and feathered, ready for winter in the Antarctic, the icy-cold season when the emperors lay their eggs.

For Ryan and Ashley and all the other birdwatchers
who may never get to Antarctica   —B. Z. G.

For Norman, who works tirelessly and selflessly for
what is just and right. With love.   —J. P.

Many thanks to Laura Godwin, Reka Simonsen, and the others at Holt
who helped with this book.

Henry Holt and Company, LLC, *Publishers since 1866*
115 West 18th Street, New York, New York 10011
www.henryholt.com
Henry Holt is a registered trademark of Henry Holt and Company, LLC
Text copyright © 2001 by Brenda Z. Guiberson
Illustrations copyright © 2001 by Joan Paley
All rights reserved.
Distributed in Canada by H. B. Fenn and Company Ltd.
Library of Congress Cataloging-in-Publication Data
Guiberson, Brenda Z. The emperor lays an egg /
Brenda Z. Guiberson; illustrated by Joan Paley.
1. Emperor penguin—Juvenile literature.
2. Parental behavior in animals—Juvenile literature.
[1. Emperor penguin. 2. Penguins.] I. Paley, Joan, ill.
II. Title. QL696.S473G85 2001 598.47—dc21 00-40980

ISBN 0-8050-6204-1 / EAN 978-0-8050-6204-5 (hardcover)
10 9 8 7 6 5 4 3
ISBN 0-8050-7636-0 / EAN 978-0-8050-7636-3 (paperback)
10 9 8 7 6 5 4 3 2 1

First published in hardcover in 2001 by Henry Holt and Company
First paperback edition—2004 / Designed by Donna Mark.
The illustrator created the collages in this book by cutting shapes
from paper that she hand painted.
Printed in the United States of America on acid-free paper. ∞